No Sign

No Sign

Poems by Sydney Lea

THE UNIVERSITY OF GEORGIA PRESS
ATHENS AND LONDON

© 1987 by Sydney Lea
Published by the University of Georgia Press
Athens, Georgia 30602
All rights reserved
Text designed by Betty P. McDaniel
Set in 10 on 13 Linotron Palatino
The paper in this book meets the guidelines for
permanence and durability of the Committee on
Production Guidelines for Book Longevity of the
Council on Library Resources.

Printed in the United States of America

91 90 89 88 87   5 4 3 2 1

Library of Congress Cataloging in Publication Data

Lea, Sydney, 1942–
No sign.
I. Title.
PS3562.E16N6 1987   811'.54   86-19160
ISBN 0-8203-0916-8 (alk. paper)
ISBN 0-8203-0917-6 (pbk.: alk. paper)

British Library Cataloging in Publication Data available.

For Robin.
    And for Jordan.

Acknowledgments

Some of these poems, occasionally in somewhat different form, appeared in the following periodicals, to whose editors the author extends his thanks.

Abatis: "Issues of the Fall"
The Atlantic: "Midway"
The Bennington Review: "The Dream of Sickness: To Landy Bartlett in Vermont"
Crazyhorse: "How to Leave Nothing," "No Sign"
The Georgia Review: "Horn," "Tough End"
The Hudson Review: "Burning the Christmas Tree"
The Iowa Review: "Waiting for Armistice"
Ironwood: "High Wind"
The Kenyon Review: "Annual Report," copyright 1987 by Kenyon College. Reprinted with permission.
Negative Capability: "Art of the Son"
The New Republic: "Fall," "Making Sense," "Sereno"
The New Yorker: "After Labor Day," "The Return: Intensive Care," "Leonora's Kitchen," "Dusk"
The Partisan Review: "The Light Going Down"
Prairie Schooner: "Yet Unharmed," copyright 1986 by University of Nebraska Press. Reprinted with permission.
The Sewanee Review: "Telescope"
Tendril: "Reckoning"
Verse: "December Seventh"
The Virginia Quarterly Review: "From Another Shore," copyright 1983 by *The Virginia Quarterly Review.*

The author would like to express gratitude to the Rockefeller Foundation for a residency at the Bellagio Study Center, during which this volume was completed; he is particularly grateful to Mr. Roberto Celli and Ms. Angela Barlmetter.

The author would also like to acknowledge the friendship, help, and support of Linda Gregerson, Jay Parini, Terry Hummer, Mark Jarman, Joey Olsen, Lynne MacMahon, Terry Lawson, Rod Santos, Maura High, Jim Schley, Stephen Arkin, Peter Woerner, and Don Metz.

Contents

IV. RECKONING

Proem

In some familiar but unnameable country
(I wanted to call it Domain of Despair-Upon-Anger)
you beat with your fists at your temples,
the red child twisting away

from the ready breast.
I wanted to fly against all propagandists
for Nature as beautiful, blissful.
What bliss in the child's crook neck?

(I thought of birds as Audubon posed them,
the way they were torqued
against arising, against decorum.)
Nothing of beauty,

unless perhaps in the barely buried crimson bloodstreams,
the boychild's plumage of tension.
I was, I suppose, a study
in guilt whenever I woke back from gliding in dream's

deep sky, where body and mind
go loose and automatic.
For what had I in me
to offer by way of atonement?

Yet something took hold in time.
By the third week he had it,
praise be to training, resolve.
I recall at last that delicious moment

when your arms dropped winglike on sheets,
and your face at last into effortless love.

"Nothing *to* it," you smiled,
like the neighbor's child who pedals past,

hands at her sides,
milk teeth glinting as morning's mists
lift into sun and summer's slowest blue.
Spring's abrasions have perfectly healed on her knees.

No longer tears to white her cheeks;
the unspeakable sadness and fury
as ground drew down her leaden body—
all gone too.

Now she casually looks
at the kingfishers, military-smart,
on their beat up and down the brook.
In and out of barns, this season's swallows arc

as if flight from the nest demanded
no more than the wish that impelled it. . . .
Something changed in us all.
Eyes grew keener in their very languor—

we watched the fontanelle
as bone began to close on the frantic flicker
of pulse, and something impeded
the hurtle of hour, day, week,

though my step felt lighter and quicker
—you two soft in sleep—
those mornings I walked the puppy,
who seemed now to heel like a dog in the movies.

It came to the single basswood
as the child lay feeding on the fourth of his Sundays:

something so brilliant, you said,
it looked almost phony.

A scarlet tanager. Outsized.
A deep-woods bird, and shy,
yet it swung back and forth in our window tree,
pretty and seemingly happy,

throughout the baby's adagio satisfaction
with your either side,
as if for all of its colorful bombast
it were simply a part of the breeze.

It couldn't last.
It wasn't supposed to be
in such an odd, unnatural location;
and yet somehow appeared resolved to stay.

I

How to Leave Nothing

Fall

Carpenter, Mechanic, and I:
it is our yearly hunting trip
to this game-rich, splendid, dirt-poor margin
of Maine. There is always rain and a gale,
and one or two
bluebird days just to break the heart.
We're good at this thing we do,
but for each bird that falls,
three get by us and go
wherever the things that get by us go.

To the realm of baby shoe and milk tooth;
kingdom of traduced early vow,
of the hedge's ghost, humming with rabbit and rodent,
under the mall's macadam. All that seemed
fixed in the eye.   I,
according to Mechanic,
is too melancoholic. Yes, says Carpenter,
and talks when he ought to be doing.
We all watch the canny Setter, with her nose
like a Geiger counter.

"There's not much gets by *her*,"
we repeat each year, admiring, after she's flashed on point
and *shaaa!*—in redundant wind another grouse flies wild.
Air and ridge and water now all take
the color of week-old blood. Or years-old ink.
We are such friends it's sad.
Not long before we stalk before winter the heavy-horned
bucks that slide past,

spirit-quiet, in spare brush.
Then Carpenter and Mechanic in their loud mackinaws will
  seem

interruptions on the skyline of the sky's
clean slate. And so will I.

Telescope

Light projected lifetimes ago
from farthest stars is arriving now
here where my poor house moans
on its chilling sills and stones;
and where I—quieter, sleepless,
with only my half-blind dog for witness,
everyone else in slumber—
stand silent before such wonders.
I know alone, and inexactly,
the inexact science of memory.
A man who studies things to come
for livelihood tells me in time
there will be a lens which, pointed back
to earth, may show us all our past,
even to our creation.
How little would be the elevation
it needed to show me the people
and places I might have considered crucial:
my young friend Michael drunkenly
hulking over his purple Harley,
rumbling murder in my driveway,
swearing against the blossoms of May
that pinkly dropped around us there
like what we might have taken for flares
of warning, if he had been less proud,
and I more equal to warning. I stood
dumb as a dog. You could call it collusion,
or guilt by reason of inaction.
With the glass I could also see the feathers
flare on a pheasant held by my father,
and the Springer who cocked her head and chattered,

and wanted to hunt, and what was the matter?
Around us the last of afternoon fell
on the last stalks standing in autumn fields
as now, by word and heart, he petitioned
me for the slightest recognition.
I wouldn't hear the argument.
I had no interest in what was meant,
his words kept rising into balloons
of white, like those things you see in cartoons
above a speaker's head.
Turn the lens a hair and he's dead,
mouth stone-rigid, heart gone bust.
And oh how slightly I'd have to adjust
the telescope in order to see
the woeful host of memory,
other scenes—not all of course
of life and death—that exact remorse:
the way a guttering candle flickers
—I simply don't know what to give her—
in the importuning eye of a girl;
my runt chum Ronnie in a whirl
of agony as I refrain
from choosing him up for some childhood team;
the whirling earth a galaxy
of scene and soul and silence and need.
A word or two, not much
beyond what I said . . . or a touch—
how little it seems it would have taken
to change the times I now imagine
in which a now quiet man or woman,
myself included, would come off better.
But all these moments are fixed forever,
and such a lens no more effective
than memory, no more corrective.

How to Leave Nothing

Elwood had said, "It's dangerous." He'd said, "Don't ride
  that way, back-looking."
And I told my brother I'd like to burn Elwood out and leave
  him nothing.
Breathing heavy, that night we plotted revenge on Elwood
  for squealing.
It is fabled, the care of assassins and thieves.

We threaded a succulent mudworm on every tine of a treble
  fish hook. Oh deftly,
we tossed the whole deception over his miserable fence, and
  patiently,
we waited. We waited, even after the line had begun to
  move.
We counted to ten, then counted again.
We gave ourselves more than all the time we needed. And
  then we yanked.

You've heard a chicken. Well, if we hadn't known that this
  was a chicken
who had gobbled down our bait, we'd have thought it was
  something else. The whole
furious pathetic swirl of hen came hurricaning over
before Elwood could scratch a match.
Before he could make a light, we lit out. "Dirty for dirty," I
  said.

Yes, we had stolen the horse. You might call it stealing.
  Elwood did.
Yes, we had ridden him backwards. You might call it riding.
  (Elwood said *racing*.)

But the horse was our lenient uncle's, and he was away, in
    the hospital,
and the horse was as old in animal years

as Elwood himself. We were plodding. Looking back. We
    liked the way
the browning meadows of summer kept falling in hindsight.
    And now I remember
liking the way the late sun fell in my brother's hair.
Now that he's gone. He was mounted before

—or was it behind?—me there. On that ride, flushing,
    rattling, falling,
grasshoppers imprecisely bordered our wake. Elwood tried
to follow, citing Commandments, feigning concern. And
    then he tattled,
and the farmer's leather strap sang.
And so we left Elwood just one of his precious two skinny
    birds,

for his false witness. We ate the second, raw for the green
    wood
we used, so blood would ooze each time that one of us
    would open
his mouth in a sneer: "So he wanted us to be careful!" Or,
    "To hell
with Elwood, anyway!" Miserable
sentimental old black with his horsehair wristlets. To hell
    with him

and his tatterdemalion chickens and gardens, his pigs and
    goats, his Bible!
To hell we agreed with the way he would always lay down
    his hoe or bucket
full of dung, and take from his pocket those sweat-stained
    pictures

—departed wives, the rickety daughter,
the son who went bad—and curse the Devil. To hell with
   the rag he reddened
with coughs and sobbed in, and wiped his hands on. To hell
   with the hands themselves
he would clasp to pray, and with the stinking cold solitary
   yam
he would eat for lunch every day! To hell

with every stinking inch of Elwood for telling, Elwood for
   whining,
"It's dangerous. Don't ride that way, back-looking."
   Kneeling, we threw the remnant
flesh and bone and feather into the fire. Oh, we took care
to leave nothing, absolutely nothing,
for Elwood or anyone else to mark us by. Still careful, we
   stood,

still watching the last of coals turn ash in the dark, we
   backed away.

After Labor Day

Your son is seven years dead.
"But it seems," I said, seeing your face
buckle in mid-conversation
as over the fields came winging the trebles
of children at holiday play—
I said, "But it seems like yesterday."

"No," you said,
"Like today."

In the first of the black fall drizzles,
in a morning when world's-end seems to hover
too near, the early fallen
leaves slick on the highway as blood,
the yellow ball had spun to a halt
on the white line:
your small child scurried there like an ignorant vole. . . .

It is the time of year
when hawks rush down the pass where you live,
but the heat last weekend held them
northward. So grounded, we talked like voluble schoolkids
inside, instead. —Or I did.
You lost in thought, dark brows arched
like the wings of birds at travel,
or soaring to hide, or seek.

At home, I recall your eagle visage, how now
and then it falls
just so. In the change, in the first cold autumn rain,
I play at identification.

I imagine how Redtail, Cooper's,
Roughleg, Little Blue Darter,
and the odd outsider—Swainson's, say—
now pass you by,
as at home in my study I watch
two scruffy starlings on a wire outside
fronting what they seem to have
no choice but to front
till one peels off, is sucked it seems into woods, and through
the glass I yet can hear him.
His croaks come this way, as if the other
were the one who had vanished, not he.

Just so lost children imagine
their parents are lost, not they.
"Where did you go?" they chirp, as if we hadn't been
shrieking, searching.
Or as if our terror had been a game.

It's the season of the mushroom all of a sudden.

Closed though my window is,
over the vapors and trees I also hear
the doubled scream of a kestrel.

You heard, these seven years have heard, the swish
of tandem tires through puddles,
the last gasps
of airbrakes, screams.
And loud as unthinkable detonation
—or so at least in dreams it seems—
the impact:

every outside sound raced clear to you.
But walls and panes cut short your shouts

from inside the house,
as if *you* were the small boy
to whom the remote roar
of the world was suddenly apparent,
yet whose voice was as in dreams
unheard or worse: irrelevant.

In the lulls, by way of compensation,
I talked the holiday away.
Talked and talked and
talked and talked
and catalogued the game:
I called attention
to early Goldeneyes out on the marsh;
to the way in later light
—like cheap raincoats—the feather's colors
on the backs of ducks would change and change;
and, higher, to the cloud that would mean this greater
    change,
swooping against the yellow ball of the sun.

As if through a shield of thin glass,
there was the further drone of the bomber whereby,
you said, "One day the world will be lost,"

and the bitter joke, I understood,
be on those of us who all these seasons
have played at discourse.
"Where did you go?"
So the world will ask.

Yet Unharmed

Not dark nor light. Such birds as fly on a day
like this have flown out of sight. No agony:
dusk had induced my will to forgetfulness
until I stumbled on these signs of violence.
I want to put it by. An owl has stooped
—snowflakes fall, are intincted with new blood—
and gone

        I'm nine. The wafers are ghosts on our tongues:
"Sing praises to His name, He forgets not His own"—
all of us in uncomfortable Sunday clothes
sing the morning verse to this puzzling close.
For isn't it odd to gather and chant His praises
for knowing His only name? But I'm too pious
to question the lyric. And outside the smoothness waits,
the redolent fire on the pond's shore warms our skates,
potatoes nestle in coals. *Thunk thunk:*
the jolly bass of air-cracks, bank to bank.
What matter that for years I've been told the truth
shall set me free?

        Crack! we set her loose.
Our youngest sister flies to the other shore,
her blades unsteady, her make-believe screams of fear
a tonic, soprano sweetness there. We children
—if we were a little older—might choose to imagine
the patience and pain of creatures in their wait
in lifeless mud. Instead we count the insects
who counted too long on protracted Indian Summer:
lodged in ice as if they were caught in amber,
like angels' hair their wings net a murky glow

17

from underneath, but from the purer clouds
above they take a color brighter than air.
We have built the fire again as we huddle here.
The sisters begin a comic round. All join,
until the words are lost in the jumble and din.
No one will speak a name; we're so familiar,
familiar *you* suffices. Mother and Father,
in such communion as this, are everlasting
as life must be. Radiant endless morning.
(Even their cryptic exchanges, *sotto voce*,
on so and so's divorce or injury
or death or tragic farce of senility:
all is blended together here. Benignly.)
This is the picture entitled, Yet Unharmed.
On the dam, a crow unravels a claret strand
from one of last fall's fish who perished at spawn.
In such a vision even his croak is tuneful.

Walter and Lewis play "Under the Double Eagle,"
the old guitar and banjo interweaving
seamlessly, the women promenading.
Who is the man who clogs, up on the table?
Onlookers smile. (Franklin, Ada, Donald,
and that logger—his name escapes me—who'll drown at
    Beartrap.)
We've driven in so slowly along the blacktop,
we and Mother (Father is gone), avoiding
the frogs reborn in the puddles, leaping, crossing,
glinting in headlamps like so many rough-cut gems
among the darker discs of their flattened friends.
The hall is dry. The clogger sips vanilla.
We've rehearsed the songs we're hearing: "Sweet Florilla,"
in which a Frenchman keens from the opposite shore
of Gaspereau for the Maine girl buried here.
"The Rusty Attic." "The Wabash Cannonball,"

in which around poor Danny the curtain falls,
but he's carried home to glory along the rails.
The clogger reels, collapses, is carried home
as Patrick's fiddle sweetly laments false dawn
and I and my youngest brother stand in the doorway:
the clogger's pathos, his shouts of "Set me free!"
blend with the peepers' choirings, tree to tree.

 The youngest brother has gone to the other side.
(To fish, that is. Not like the other, to die.)
I hear his wordless singing as it reaches
here become a part of seamlessness
—sky, lake, rock, beach, mountain—
within which one whom I call *I* claims freedom.
The irksome insects of August have given over.
The oaks above me are barely touched with umber,
a hue like sherry's. I loll on a mossy stone
and gaze oblivious up into a crown.
September. Evening and autumn set to come,
savors I can almost feel on the tongue.
Cumuli rally themselves away to the east
over Three Dawn Mountain, dark among its trees,
light in the clearings. What would a free thought be?
What are my worn clichés? Born Yesterday.
Yet Unharmed. Proof Against All Change.
I name the other peaks, the encompassing range,
without a look, my eyes still lifted up
among the leaves, from which there breaks a shape
—color of dusk that is at last no color—
at last veering off to carry off something other.

 For all the languor, sweetness I would sing,
recalling my own, I feel the wind of that wing.

II

Issues of the Fall

Issues of the Fall

All the plenitude of a sudden so changed! Like quick cartoons of a thought,
a feeling. Small beasts turned milk-white from brown. Pale in air,
fluff—the lingering milkweed pinwheels off. High up,
fern blackens where buck and doe are getting
ready: he scents the musk at her light-
haired whorl of entry. Risen,
darkened goslings
chuckle,
mourn
in pairs. And so on.

I'm thinking of animation, and these last statements of consequence
from old Summer: tried as the 'pecker's scarcening jabs, thumps
at a long season's end. Hollow. Bored. But it's deep,
it is almost infernal, the time restored
to the speeding mind by such a time,
each year repeated as now
it's repeated before
the curtain
falls
again. Of snow.

Before into new and back. Old into after. I speak of transformation,
my own and others: A childhood theater, Disney, and my Mother
ceasing to be merely Mother, but not yet another
woman, fantasy so altering the very nature
of things that I and the world might
fall through the vortex—so
frequent a figure
in the moving
pictures—
I to become

23

fowl or animal. Gifted with the power to speak in defiance of all
I had been taught to think was true, was natural. I would learn
the words, moves. "You don't even know down from up,"
an older girl had told me in an early hard
day at school. The liquid sound
of kisses above me like
the suck of straws
at milkshakes,
Good
and Plenty, spare evil

scent that dropped from the balcony. I mustn't ever climb there! Why, then,
did they call it "colored Heaven"? On the screen, locked in an embrace,
Mickey and Minnie sigh, chuckle at Pluto, Pluto
somehow swallows a whistle. There's a cry
from deep inside: someone older
might imagine the far wail
of a soul on its way
to hell.
Hard
laughter down dark

air. Which I will join, damnation be damned! Or salvation. And yet it's far
from funny, it's frightful, this sad high summons from low beastly bowels,
attended by beasts. I tremble, but long to rise or tumble
among them. Mother coaxes me back to silence,
briefly. The camera's tricks make up
a finale: buds transformed
to pale angels, whirling
earthward,
taking
on animal guise.

There are rare tears in Mother's eyes at these wonderful speeding frames.
Uncertain how to respond, I whistle. The milk of childhood drains.

The Light Going Down

The worms crawl in, the worms crawl out,
The worms play pinochle on your snout. . . .
   My daughter and the schoolfriend who looks like her,
tuneless and cheerful, repeat the old ditty on Death—
pale Music-master who has not yet entered
the mind to insist on the tune.

They can't imagine what it will be
to recall from somewhere back not knowing the Master.
   I can. And go on imagining:
how would it be to go on living
backwards always, beginning
with Death? To rise from his recital room
in censure and pain, born of undying?

How brief the time
before one cast aside the cane, the crutch, and walked
   ever more into the upright,
and to hell with the Bingo, the card games!
One would feel the cloth swell taut
again over arm and thigh
and groin. A backing to bloom.

One's lifemate, assuming such good fortune,
would grow in this version more easy with every moment
   to comprehend and to love with abandon
till it seemed the two of you lay
pooled in the sweat of intimacy
forever. How would that be,

such comfort before the tears
(so useless for years) that poured
　　at oddest hours, at slightest slights?
Then a horde of children hurtling (though ever more slowly)
beside you back to school, to the moments of flood
as your first love told you love had faded
before the early words of ardor sank in the playground
　　ruckus.

Then a drawn-out unlearning
of word and figure, the telling of time.
　　By now Eternity must loom,
especially summers, the elders below
chewing their words and foods on a creaking porch,
night locusts calling back another daytime.

Life must drag, everlasting,
each year a larger fraction,
　　a term you no longer had the meaning of. . . .
Imagining, one saddens
at the prospect of Love unravelled
and the slow unknowing

of Death, whose tenor had husked one's every testament
of affection and anger,
　　until one lived oneself back past ditty
and farther. Through Mother Goose,
nonsense rhyme, to the wordless

wail of straightforward desire
as one wormed one's way to the Woman's belly,
the light going down,
and yet one knew,
from back somewhere,
how quiet it would be, how comfortless, there.

The Art of the Son

His father feels
anger, fear, grief and remorse
mixed as on a palette when he wakes
to *thump* and *thump,* the earthquake bass downcellar
amid the heaps and clouds
of smoke that are the son's room;
when he wakes to amplified lyrics. The words *kill*
and *death* appear liturgical. . . .

From the heaps of apparent cloud
that had been the son's early drawings
at length emerged the shapes of beast and machine
and man and woman
that the world might credit,
quaking with recognition,
for they seemed to signal such violence.
Just so,

from what had been the flesh of a child,
soft and vague,
cable and cantilever and pan
of muscle in the boy's body
—they seemed at length to signal violence—
slowly articulated themselves.
The father whispered,
Behold a man!

He imagines his son downstairs
now studying one of his favorite subjects
in the long hallway mirror,
beholding, vague with chemicals, a man.

Whose had been that poverty the boy felt?
Whose but his own, when his figures begged for features?
When his trucks heeled always away from the upright
and houses tilted marginward?

Though it's one of his favorite subjects
—the cruel mutability of things,
the way they shift, explode,
at the very moment when you hope to hold them—
nothing could be made right
by a father's words. And so the boy would destroy them,
bombarding his drawings with color, tearing the sheet,
his theme now rage. Not yet abated.

His father would utter solace and hold him,
but little wonder, he shifted away
from everything that a parent craves
in his childish romance of childhood.
His province became and is
the world laid waste.
Now his father imagines him
studying his face, the one eye

scarlet and black,
the lips distended over a coppery taste
of blood in his smile.
He has done an even prettier job on his rival,
and now imagines him,
his pained face, wasted.
He might just love his father
simply to storm

down and yank at his spiked scarlet hair.
Let him try it. . . .
How is it, his father wonders,

that this careless child infers
wealth from annihilation, as if death were dollars?
Where did he go wrong, mis-speak himself?
He thinks of an April dawn,
coppery, frozen, after untimely storm,

when the boy woke him to drifts of dead tanagers
strewn on the lawn like so many careless dollars.
He thinks of how he spoke
about the world
squandering beauty,
about how prodigality
might be a part of beauty's meaning.
Was it from then

that the "bombs" of scarlet and black
became at once more common and fierce,
scarring the paper
in the small boy's renderings,
meaning demanding exorbitant meanness?
Had he been wrong on another morning
to laugh at prodigality
when his son roused him to see "the pretty money"?—

a paycheck the boy had decked with rainbow arcs and x's.
Or to hold his tongue on yet another
when the boy held up a portrait
of three vermilion kittens and said,
"They're my best waste ever.
They're dead."
And was all this an innocence or meanness?

Thump and *thump:* the bass beneath his bed.

Waiting for Armistice

Under Aunt Alice's
table, its skirts of chiffon
pulled to, the little man
played at his sullenness.

            He had been lightly
punished, whatever
his sin, enjoined to act gentle
from this day on. It was partial
darkness he sought,
now and forever.

          From the GE above
he heard the broadcast nightly
news, and then the Ink Spots'
baritone crooned
"I want a Sunday
kind of love."

         He wanted summer,
under the roundelay
of tern and cloud,
his aunts in that season
in long-skirted dresses,
blowing him kisses,
rounding their blood-colored mouths
to please him.

        Aunt Alice,
his favorite, had caught

for him the lead
ring on the sideshow carousel
at a one-ring circus—
good enough.

                Now, as he hid,
she sang along.
Sweet trills!
though here and there she gasped,
went rough,
as she had that time when his Mother
held her tight
and keened and moaned:
"Don't cry. You'll have another."

                "A love to last
past Saturday night. . . ."

                Impossible
there, in his put-up remorse,
to imagine the blue
pushpin standing for Uncle
Dick ripped out
of the wall-map, and Alice
done with her morning reports
on the Allies' progress;
with her modest ladylike shouts
of gusto after the news
till this March: '45.

                How to imagine then
the other husbands later,
home, alive?
All heroes. Strangers.

                    There would stand
his own father
in the June sphere of light
that fell on the drive
just before night
fell on the house of the women. . . .

                    How to imagine
these women decamped,
the lush perfumes of bereft
Alice and Grandmother,
and of the spinster aunts
—Olive and Myrtle—
and finally of Mother
herself, dragged off
in the winds?

                    How imagine his future
brothers, battles,
when the closest harmony reigned?
Lisped trebles at bed
and at meals. And for his sickness
his choice of the softest
sensitive hand
to tamp away the runnels
of sweat from his head.

                    And for his wickedness,
whips laid on like wands.
Sweetness of female indulgence,
forgiveness, unearned!
                    The satin skin
of the afternoon bay
that summer would always return
to the light-soaked cottage

in an even gentler way
its ever-so-gentle image,
forever in mind
wedded to the tunes of Tin Pan Alley—
"You must have been a beautiful baby,"
and all the battalions
of others,
even sweeter,
and the hopeful smiles of that season.

Wasn't there blood? O maybe . . .
O surely! But it was hidden,
the one thing unshared.

Every day a Sunday,
so that these women
in their refugee camp
(the same old radio bears the word,
nearly forty years gone by)
—their clothing yanked
away, their lives—
bring on the selfish little man's tears,

but there's no safe place to hide.

—AFTER THE PHALANGIST MASSACRES IN BEIRUT

December Seventh

My wife and I exchange parts
of the old saw:
Like being beaten on the head with a club . . .
It feels so good when it stops.
Gales from all quarters
hustle last night's snow
into a maze of airborne horizontals.

It feels so good to think of shelter—
furnace, lamp and wick lit up
the brief day long—
and then to go back in.
The retriever and spaniel
prance on the steely crust
while the little basset pokes along,

prophet-faced, in the tracks we leave.
It's the dormant season for trees,
but their sleep seems restless:
we hear the irregular snores of one,
as if of someone old who has seen too much
of comings in and goings out,
and rolls and tosses,

and the mutters and whines of a pair whose cold limbs
    touch,
like those of a couple, once lovers,
who now all through the night
do battle for space, for pillow and covers.
Where are the chickadee bravos

who manage to stay all winter?
They must be clinging with their tiny talons

to any thing that remains,
unbelievably, still in such storm.
We stagger a little farther.
We are tinkering with pain,
making the notion of home,
with every step, greater and warmer.
Wonder of human making!

Butcher, baker, candlestick maker:
red bacon and bread on the table, the sconces casting
a uterine glow.
A blade to reduce the forest to board.
Drill exacting oil's ebony flow.
Tank truck's rubber wheels.
Combine threshing the stone-free field.

So loud out here. So cold.
In hibernation, beasts' hearts will slow
to nearly a halt
while we pour out our hearts in beloved chatter
within a Japanese box of temperance and affection:
this house, this storey, this living room and kitchen.
Parent and child.

Lover and lover.
Over the scraping of limb on limb,
of wind on land
and wind on wind;
over the silent begging of dogs
who have had enough and tend to their kennel,
this roaring. . . .

We signal our pets to heel. We tremble.
It's only a local lumberman, skidding out logs
on this ghastly morning.
His head held rigid to the purpose,
he doesn't see us here below.
His smoke vent gushes
a fume to which the flakes are blown

and turn to black water.
Sheep chew mutely their cuds near Alamagordo.
Raising their barrels of heads, the buffalo
watch the jellied rain take hootch and ground.
Cats feel the air with whiskers as porcelain shivers
and falls from the shelves of Dresden.
Perhaps less shrieking than animal quiet in Warsaw,

people regarding each other like cattle bludgeoned.

Making Sense

A tatting of wings this morning
broke silence, and dream:
a spider tethered a wasp to a mullion.
I tried, failing,
to resist my own translation—
Just as the field growth arrays
itself in summer seed-fringe, it seems,
each thing in its way
begins to prepare
for winter, inside and out.
The kingdoms below us all season
have eaten and given
themselves to be eaten without
remark or record, have known fears
and lusts but not
as a man might know them:
as nooses
mounted the wings in a silken
skein, to spider and wasp,
there occurred
perhaps some version
of *Here is an end*
of all this.
Don't call it neurosis.
Their vibrations
were routine,
professional, unlike those
of a man,

one who sees how the knuckles of one hand
have turned to white onions,

and picks at his food, and
looks out the windows
through the light
spare rain.
He is inside.
Try to project
him seated there as the panes
begin with the night
to close off the pond, barn, cornpiece, the last few
nighthawks slicing the last few
ephemerids from air.
As the glass collects
the dark and dew
and reflects
his small sequestered dwelling's contents
back upon him, like conscience,
or simple consciousness,
try to picture him there.
Try to imagine him try
to make nothing
of all this, to make sense
of his day, his situation,
by making outward sense
an alternative to meditation:
sight, the great turtle
he confronted when, at dawn, he pried
the hatch of his well,
and deeper in, the gutted carp in the pool;
by noon, he could *smell*
wine in the wind off windfall apples
where late-laid larvae will die;
touch, in late afternoon,
when the lame hand brushed a spit bug's drool;
the bug's unlikely whistle
will do for *sound*,

heard before supper; for *taste,*
his recall
now of an odd flavor like charcoal
in the scarred skin over his late wife's
late left breast.
For all of which the word is *Trouble,*
trouble, trouble! Not a growth from
the ground, but the ground itself
of self, which will not leave
all this alone.

I want the old man's grief
to be the winter-silent pain
of the body alone.
I want the old man older than I
to lend authority.
I want him to have learned by the end
of all this to make sense
no more than sense.
But see the hand
tense, like something that wants to take flight.
The spider has long since
retreated into sleep,
the wasp hanging
drugged in his casing.
Without comment.
Forever quiet.
But listen.
The old man will speak.
He is inside.
He will go on speaking,
I fear, into the night.

Tough End

There is no place without them,
these scourges of sense and mind. Always
on the farther reach of some divide.
When we had trains, we'd say
the other side of the tracks.
Now it's *across the brook,* or *past the Town Land,*
or *over the mountain.*
        We call our own Tough End,
though its function of marking
an end is vague:
the middle of nowhere, and not
a finale of anything physical. Almost like dreams
to us, these dirt yards thronged with tires,
one painted white containing
the ghostly stalk of some crude flower,

        like a far-gone drunk,
somehow still standing, poking through ashen snow.
And next to it a fridge in trance, or a dryer,
among the car and pickup wrecks.
A kind of domicilic
code of dress, everywhere honored that's country—
I've seen it in Illinois, in Georgia, in the dust-
thrashed hamlets of Canada's grain states,

        south and north. All you need is a border.
Redneck baroque: platoons of bound and scrawny
hound-mix dogs that quake,
free-running poultry, and inside, children
who also shiver, dirty and doughy and bruised

denizen genies of the canted trailers,
sheds, or whatever. (I could tell you
of tincan cabins, piano crate porches,

        but you've seen them too. . . .)
The realm not only of style but also of story.
We speak the tales we know about our Tough End
in our bars, so cool and quiet, so clean, and so
unlike their yowling honkytonk dives
named *Fuzzy Duck,* or *Breakdown Alley,* and such,
or called by their owners' brusque singular handles:
Duke's. Dick's. Pat's. Pete's. Jake's. Joe's.

        As if in contest,
we make up our fables, each invented to top
the other, we tell them well and with rising passion,
as if we were participants
in all their outrage so long as we keep on talking,
Tough End a kind of muses' haunt
and each of us a bard.   Is it a realm of demons?
Or just the plastic stuff

        of whatever we fashion,
sitting so. We go there—over the line—in mind
alone. Each of us knows the legends:
Gyp Smiley's store of arms
discharging itself into ceiling and sky
as his cabin blackened, the firemen afraid
to leave their trucks. Or Horace Tutt's
manner of punishing children—cigar burns,

        scalding water, or furious shoves
from hayloft to ground.
Or each of the four Hyde brothers
in celebration of Independence devouring

a fresh-killed fawn.
The legends get old and banal,
and so we chuckle, laugh, howl, grimace, strain, flush
with labor of vision and imagination—

       their wars, their murder & mayhem,
unspeakable erotics behind the veil
that Tough End draws about itself like haze
that gathers over their coal- and woodstoves,
over broken wall and burning roof and prodigious unlawful
   feast.
Or like that curtain of rage
its citizens close on themselves as they go
—wine-sick, tobacco-hoarse—incredibly

      back before we rise every day
to labor in mill, road, woodlot, field.
The closest we come to such heat is delicious frenzy
in our narration. When the spell is done,
we shake our heads,
and wish them all in hell,
as if . . .
as if we wished Tough End would vanish,

      and we might live without them.

Burning the Christmas Tree

The old year flown, and a new one revolved:
the vivid toys assimilated,
the once-used ribbons spooled and saved,
the others disposed of, that use had faded.
This yearly try after holiday
to kindle a spirit that hadn't quite been
sufficiently there. My brothers and I
and later my sisters: all standing in
what, in that season, should always have been
a dazzle of snow.
                          The Garden Eros
—blinded both by nature and weather—
upheld a tray whose portion of frost
gripped the single shaft of a feather.

A first match stuttered and died in the breath
of the wind. Our own breaths shot from the yard
like startled quail. From underneath
Father's mild oaths, imperfectly heard,
at length a minuscule needle would flare,
and then in time we heard the crackle
(like the crumple of gift paper—partridges, stars
inscribed thereon). Each year this ritual,
not then so known, impelling tears
in memory now.
                          Like the stab of a gale.
All Christmas burned as we hugged each other,
brother, father, sister, mother.
The quick flames stripped our tree to a quill.

III

Midway

The Light

There's Boyhood's House. White sill and sash, gray stone.
My room is ever my room. I pause at the turn
on the way from school, its autumn fields, my cracked
ribs and trampled hands: the home lights mark
the turn as days contract, and gleams contract
to nugget size, perfect, clear as sparks.
Now I may enter. . . . The Early Marriage House
is a lamp itself: fog-yellow paint, a naked
bulb fixed awkward to the porch's clapboard
muted by generations of hell-bent moths.
House on a hill—a climb from the job, that ground
on which I find it's always fourth and long.
(I'm young, and cull my metaphors from games.)
Light diffuses itself to room after room,
once the children—departing the dark—have come.
Although that marriage gutters, it's a home.
It somehow *is*. There is in newer life
The Newer House as well. New child, new wife,
new lights that swim in spring in dampened splendor
through mists and rains. As if they could recover,
body and mind . . . perhaps the world has room
for every soul and thing. I pause at the turn.
It's winter. Light that falls on the driveway gravel
dazzles every rock and clod and fissure.
And now I recall a tale from the family Bible
(whose inky middle pages link the Scriptures,
New and Old, and make a gazeteer
of deaths and births and weddings, year on year):
When the seventy elders led by Moses and Aaron
saw God, they saw beneath His feet a pavement
like sapphire stone, like the very heaven for clearness.

Within, old bodies and minds collide, but harmless;
for the moment there is no place in the world for
    bereavement.
There is light. The darkness has not overcome it.
Parents, children, brothers, sisters play
within a house of yellow, white and gray,
house candescent there upon its summit.
House on a hill, my room forever my room,
and ever light within to bring me home.

Leonora's Kitchen

—AFTER, AND FOR, ERIC LARSEN

Imagine we do not know that she was so young,
that she encountered a sudden illness and fell,
gone out to the hencoop to gather eggs
for Sunday night's light supper.
The men and her boys are in town.
In the simple kitchen, the radio stutters with lightning
that flashes far off, near the station.
On the table in the middle of the room
stands a colander of beans,
red tomatoes that sweat on the oilcloth's design,
the cloth translucent
in every crease, it has been there so long.

The light is peculiar,
as if some realist painter had found a method
with light that holds the painting's mystery.
The scene can't yet be informed
by any particular pathos—
we haven't learned she lies out there,
the white hens walking idly near her,
stepping now and then across her ankles.
We cannot yet be moved to picture
one of them perched for a time on the swell of her hip,
cocking its head, spreading its meager
feckless wings and jumping down.

And the kitchen itself: it seems to do nothing
but replicate the kitchen in any house
of the country working poor,
framed as it is by porch pillars, bowed,

a floor bowed up,
a ceiling down.

The light is the apparent light of southern
Illinois on any of fifty or sixty
humid evenings, from far away
the flashes of heat.
Soon the moths will tattoo the screens,
beige on rust. She hasn't been discovered,
so the fact that she was young, was pretty and decent,
cannot mean anything yet,
if in fact it will ever mean anything.
We can't imagine in this moment
the room illuminated by anything

like that aura said to rise off the spirit rising.
Yet somehow, still, it is radiant,
and moves us, though unmoving.

The Dream of Sickness:
To Landy Bartlett in Vermont

To whom do I turn
for understanding if not to you
who with me turned from the gun dog locked on point;
from the big trout's dimpling rise;
from the chop of a hound, down in a chilly greengrove,

to look back over the land we had connected
to be here now,
where meaning seemed to be?
To whom if not to you?
I have travelled here to Ontario this August.

At home, the air
has stood on end for weeks,
full of exhaust, the mountains milky,
the condominiums sprouting like steeple bush.
Whom do I know there? What *is* "there"?

Here, already loons are bunching.
A clean wind cuffs both bay and open water,
white waves everywhere.
A month ahead of us,
the weather

puts me in mind of you, of us, of woods—
the asters at the edge of cover
freezing brown from blue; the last bees' hums;
the rodents gorging berries just before
they're sundered from the stalk—

dark smears on mulch and trail.
When I say *we*, that's what I see,
you know. And all I haven't time to list,
as if a catalogue would do:
the long hikes home, bone-weary,

feather, scale, skin, blood
annealed to one another and you and me;
conversant love for all that got away,
for where it was (wherever): for the promise
of other days in which our heart

might read, according to old habit,
slough and stream and draw and sidehill—
those places rich with possible surprise,
which wasn't, after all our years, surprise
so much as something that held its charge

and graced our dedication.
We watch those places die.
And even all this way above Toronto,
above the lesions of miserable railside shanties,
above the perishing farms

and the second growth of spindled softwood—
even here (this *up* that for so long
has been our dream of last resort),
the power launches snarl their disregard
of our old friend and hex the wind,

and red pines show the shiny scars
that trail bikes skin.
Landy: so much to talk about.
And nothing.
Like everyone,

I guess I've looked
for what's called recreation,
even as heart and mind go sick.
For what is left to us
whereby we might create again

all that held us there
where twenty years ago one heard at dusk
the whirr of farm machines
and the quizzy calls of evening birds alone?
All that held us together?

Even after dark last night
the wind persisted. I lay in a cabin,
long hours,
inhaled the jab of air with pine upon it,
took in the wail of loons that mourned for fish.

imagined myself—all terror-driven—
coursing against my will
to that gaggle of glaring lights on the southern shore
among which tape cassettes blared out
a dozen songs at once,

each like the other,
steady electric backbeat basses
shivering boughs, the understory empty
now of pelt and feather and breath.
I in a papery slip of canoe.

In the dream that came at last, your death was coming,
yet I thought it mine as well, for we
—as there you lay, and I found myself unable
to utter a single sound—
we felt something close on our camp.

We is a compact.
We, the name of that frail cabin.
We, an organism composed
of softwood needle, alder bush, elliptic
aspen stem that surrenders the leaf in storm,

the leaf that falls, the others that fell
to the triumph of autumn
that we might see
—if only in that culminating moment—
the cagey grouse or buck or snowshoe hare

as it courses a forest alley.
We, a mode of reading.
In the pure clear rain.
In the apple-tartened breeze
that is partly pain, part of the composition.

Against such reading the written word
seems nothing—either a shot or cast that misses
or kills the prey for good,
the prey that will not rise again
as ours did all those seasons,

the single bird, beast, fish an avatar,
the next a recreation,
and the next and next and next.
You lay there, single-bodied, mute with illness.
Nor could I speak, nor make connection.

Your hair, uncanny blond still in your forties,
is uncannily the shade, exact,
of fall-kissed marsh grass on an ancient morning
when the Blackducks chuckled,
looked our decoys over, came.

Your skin's the tawn of that hill just after sun
presented itself again
after we'd huddled, joked and recollected
those hours out of storm
beneath a generous spruce,

or the flank of a trout
from living in clean sand.
And you were dying.
To whom if not to you
will I turn for understanding?

You were dying.
And everywhere the whirl and clack
of some army coming.
Your heart and mind are turf and stone
and fur and freshet and down,

yet in a dream
they ticked like tires over asphalt seams,
rushing to and from
some wretched city.
Ticked toward Death.

Awake, what solace?
I felt for the phone,
but what would we do?
Repeat our litany
of ready interpretation:

how much of this seems personal attack,
backhoes draining the marshes, their rootings
as if some evil demon yanked our hair;
the scar of Jeep and trail bike on a limb
as if our skin were peeled and burning;

the slick-tongued deejay in the dancing club
maintaining his chatter
over the tink and chunk
of ice in high-priced tumblers
while heart and mind detect a demon,

and not that *genius loci*
who was a whiff of presence
above that *we*—that you-and-me,
and dog   game   rain
gun   fish   sun;

protest as I do here that love
that's not enough,
our spirits so bound up in things
we cannot here or there or ever
make again;

or simply attend
the buzz of tension wires beneath our words
that race along the lanes
—all highways now, all crowded
with hurtling chrome and steel—

before we're disconnected.

Horn

You always named it
the long way for some reason:
shell of a conch,
syllables that scanned
like *son of a bitch,*
though it was only
as angry as you
ever got. Not very. No,
Father: sad. Sad, then still;
and I can't tell you how
much sadder-sounding now.

You blew, it mourned
something, it wound
through secret paths
that I and my brothers—all
living then—had made
like qualifications
in the syntax of a man
reluctantly becoming
a realist. It knew
no abbreviation,
but tongued each
leaf, each stone
as it cozened us home.

We would come home slow, though,
for it wasn't the porchbell's
paratactic clamor,
expletive of terror:
Death! Drowning! Fire!

All rare
in recollection, though each
has been spoken for later.
An apparently casual
call, unchildlike, summons
to bed or meal, incidentals
in a lengthy period. We ambled
therefore, pausing
to imagine fatal
cooperheads on ledges, staring
at the high ridge
with its flecked aura
of buzzards, nudging
a great toad, trying out
new risky words. . . .

Let me render the sound. I can.
It held even then
the pain we feel
when we must
turn to what we have
no choice but to turn to.
Resignation's
utterance, born into us,
inflection alone
remaining to be
recalled and apprehended. Not
the percussive of lust
or catastrophe, not
the quick announcement,
midnight
phone call, bowel-shivering news
of a lover's unfaith, not
the heart-freezing

instant of diagnosis
but protracted
unease for which
the diagram is there
from the start, and on which
we gradually heap
our meanings, as flesh avails
itself of the articulate frame. Not
the hiss of the snake,
then, but as if
—in the ear's eccentric funnels—
his sound were the echo
of his body's shape,
near-comatose on the bone-
warming rocks of noon.
Or the buzzard's oritund
glidings spelled
lethargic long vowels:
"Come HOME, Come HOME. . . ."
Or the toad's pace
determined the meter
of our steps
homeward to the low
windings of the shell.

Not, therefore, shock
but circumlocution
of somberer fear:
slow homing,
meandering and glissando
of the conch's husk
the muddled signals of young
nemesis borne into later life
and named: vagueness,

collapse of margins, clarity
absent as night
comes on.

As night came on that night
when you beckoned
over and over,
but each time it seemed
from a different quarter,
as if you had entered the shadow-
flesh of the night-
jar whose call
imprecisely parses woods
and meadows, so is a dream
that shifts just
as you reach its stop.

Some knowledge
it may have been that stopped you
from clattering the bell.
The reluctance of summer
light in its dying? Awareness
of what we would later
plead? "We were trying. . . ."
Easy sentence, come to be juxtaposed
now, as I put the horn
to my lips, blow
into it forty angry years,
and all they've cost: obscenity,
imperative, then the wailed
feckless interrogative
summons. And still,
you are lost.

The Return: Intensive Care

—IN MEMORY OF DAVID FIELD

I felt for the button. . . .
There's a circle of perpetual occultation
at the depressed pole
within which stars never rise,
and at the elevated one, one of apparition
from which they never fall.
I used these facts
to figure the limits of my situation
—mine? or was it yours?—
as again I came back.

Where was I? . . .
I thumbed the button for your floor.
It lit.
Suddenly, I thought,
everywhere there are circles,
as in some new weather or fashion:
the breasts both of a young farmgirl
and, sadder, of a fat old orderly
riding up beside me;
the elevator's orbicular lampbulbs;

and, the color of linen,
each drop of snow the night before,
big and round as a saucer—
a night such as we persist in
calling a freak, though it isn't
anything more than the cycling back of things
too cursedly familiar.
Yes, though it was spring,

though it was April,
the moon had worn a great wet halo.

Signifying what?
Why look up
the facts on charts?
How often in history
has everything happened!
The nurse again wheeled away
your tray with its apple, untouched,
and two dark plums
which precisely matched,
in color and conformation,

the raccoon rounds
of valor and of exhaustion
through which your eyes peered,
brighter, still, than any planet.
O *Jesus Jesus Jesus Jesus!*
inwardly I cried,
to me the word
recurring like any old habit.
Poor stately Jew, forgive the helplessness
that enforced my genteel outward mode

as you lay there,
my smalltalk Yankee palaver
of mercilessness in Mother Nature—
buds in remission,
pathetic birds
spiralling up from the sheeted roads
as if—I surmised—nothing now remained
but vertical migration.
I dropped my eyes. All else, anything
that I might have been moved to say,

anything that might have reached to the heart
of what we may or may not be
here on earth
to do or serve, dismayed
and frightened me.
I couldn't speak
of anything beyond the trivial,
by horror of risk held back,
by horror of saying something
even more banal.

You were on morphine.
You who for the length of this evil illness
had never complained
but had made for yourself a figure
—*Look to the light,*
or *Don't try to cling. . . .*
Shy of prayer,
desperate with my own feckless
impulse to speech, at length I hung
as if in mid-air

as the dark outside
began again its round.
All so cursedly dignified!
At length, in the distilled absence of sound,
I recalled my *why why why why why!*
at the death of my small terrier.
What a petty thing to remember!
And yet perhaps those yelps
when I was so young
were the only eloquence possible.

As was perhaps the gentle rejoinder
(she had seen more than I)

of my mother's mother:
Revelation helps.
There in the hospital,
lacking for words to tender,
I had recourse to fashion.
Forgive me, I nattered;
then left, once more pushing the button;
then lifted my eyes,

searching a sign of perpetuation.
Would it do any good to tell you that I cried?
There were stars, or there were none,
from wherever it was I stood.
There was, or there wasn't, a moon.

High Wind

—IN MEMORY OF GEORGE MACARTHUR

The northwester rolls the lake the full ten miles,
and out of it falls
that sense—it's almost air—of things he spoke of.
That same wind kept us
landlocked: the prospect in such a gale was not
to move all day.
We sat and talked and sat and talked, the whiskey
anesthetic, clouds
flinging impalpable shades over cape and bay,
pines dipping east,
popple leaves on the far shore essence of silver.
Our canoes high-beached,
time looked long and steady as the blow itself.
A seeming. Words—

not these alone return to make the spell,
but the tremble as well
of things stored down so deep too often
I believe them lost
as he, forever befogged. Dream-hoards
—not thought, not willed—
merely somehow arrived. . . . Loon-cries,
a certain scent,
a slap of waves on a sea-wall. This morning,
the high wind making
its first reach across what was just now calm,
I see in the lake,
brightly rebounding every sally of sun,
a minuscule

double-end canoe, its paddler desperate
bent for progress.
And settling down—or is it a welling up?—
like some narcosis,
this trance in which I remember an older man
himself remembering:
"When they made the new canoes, the metal ones,
they looked all wrong,
but I got one anyway, for April trapping.
I liked those times.
You had some life. You weren't dead of cold,
but it still had heft,
the air; there still was ice along the shore;
and frozen rocks,

the solidest thing God made. The metal held,
but they were light,
those boats, somehow. They wouldn't take the moisture
like the wood ones do,
especially when they're older. . . ." He'd pour another,
smiling wide:
"You and me: we take the moisture too."
O how real
the seasons in his telling: gestures of hand
conjuring water
glassed at dawn, or the tangible moon at night,
or muskrats heavy
as stones in the hull, stars as thick as seeds
sown in the wake.

"But O! that second year the high wind blew
all spring, the game
seemed vanished into air. There's nothing in it—
the wind don't care
which way it's going, but if it goes against you,

you sure care.
Mornings were a fight uplake for nothing,
and evenings felt
like some big spell, that metal boat high-riding
light as froth
and empty, nothing to show, and nothing now
but a lot of wind. . . ."
The *now* he spoke of, sitting so, is *then.*
The mind returns

to the paddler out on the lake. He takes a stroke
against the two
the wind keeps gathering back until, relenting,
he shies and rides
from sight the other way, he is blown away
like the nearly human
calls of loons, the prematurely fallen
leaves, the waves
and swallows and hours and all the northern odors
that stab the brain.
Out of the high wind rolling the lake has dropped
all this that turns
from recollection to word and at last to cloud.
The world is ether.

Sereno

—7 DECEMBER 1982

Month when my cord to the womb was cut, yet almost hot
this wind, all strung with ducks, with Oldsquaw, Bufflehead
and Whistler. And the ones I'm after—high,

The clever Blacks, who stretch their necks, and circle, and
     light
out of my range for good. There was a time
this might have prompted anger, and anger self-contempt:

What was I doing here, blue feet and fingers blocks like
     wood,
the very moisture of my eyes iced over, and icebergs in my
     blood?
My blood flows easier with age, the rage to question

Faltering. Like useless thoughts, the trash-birds strafe my
     blind.
My poor dogs whine: why does the gun stay silent?
Because, as I can't tell them—because I simply watch

The nobler ducks catch whiteness off the sun,
which grows these days each day more rare,
and the bay's best blue. Parade of change.

The wind from the north is warm, is wafting
forgiveness here. To noble and ignoble.
Here on Frenchman's Cove on a spit of land, and blinded,

In this strangely torpid season I forgive
the bullies and the bullied, everyone and -thing
who wants to live, that wants to live,

The chasers and the chased:
the killer put to death today by Pentothal injection,
Charlie Brooks in Texas;

I forgive the injectors;
I forgive the intractable shyness of all secrets,
like the ducks that stay far out of range.

I forgive all beings in their desperation:
murdered, murderer; mothers, fathers wanting something
the children they bring forth can't give;

Myself for my own childhood cruelties—
the way I taunted Nick Sereno
(*serene,* a thing that neighbor never was,

Dark hungry victim, bird-boned butt of my deceptions . . .
the time I decoyed him out onto the raft
and cut him loose, and jumped.

I cut the frail hemp tether, and off he drifted, quacking fear).
And I forgive the fact that cruelty can circle:
grown, he paid me back one night in a steaming gin mill.

O, this balm of sun!
As if a lifetime's bruises might be balmed.
O, that summer would at last outlast the things to come!

Out on the flooding shellfish beds the Scoters pinwheel,
as if in fun and not in search of food.
I can even forgive the fighter pilots flying

Low as Harriers across the headland.
They flush the drifting Blacks in fear toward me.
In the hot breeze, I can count their single feathers,

Black and blue as birth,
with a seeming whiteness underneath.
Again my sweet-souled dogs look up, perplexed.

They champ their still undulled white puppy teeth.
There is more to all of this than I allow.
Here, in this paradox of weather--

Here for now I let things go,
the mind as light as light upon the wind,
as if here changed and changed into an answer.

Dusk

Mans lyfe, for to be like a smoke or
shadowe, is not only knowen to learned men. . . .

What do I know? Random birds. The trees.
I've split old cedar for the backyard fireplace:
in April I and my eight years' daughter made it,
our mortar so loosely mixed I remember it ran
out under the mold—in spite of my efforts to hold it—
whose wood now kindles the purposeless fire I burn.
Intent on book or doll inside, the girl
is silent. Shadowed, I stand out here alone.

Not quite. I lay a split of birch on the coals,
heartwood from two trees I couldn't save,
the roots all ruined; like pages off-white with age,
the paper bark curls back on itself in the heat.
There rise in smoke the gestures of vanished friends.
There in the clashing plaids of cap and shirt
is one who makes that odd toss, underhand,
building a fire as he goes. I imitate it.

Or try, as I have tried for years, and fail.
What is lost? Don making ready the coffee,
George and I kicking those little holes
of conversation in sand, our hunger sated,
belts let out. An ignorant boy of twenty,
I inwardly chafe at the way they study the flame,
the older others. George has arms like cable
strung to the knotted hands with which he points:

at the head of the lake, a barely discernible eagle.
Don shuffles the kettle. His spectacles glow.

The canoes run up on the beach can be hauled down,
and then, I think, God knows where we might go! . . .
Those boats were light as steam and green as lawn,
where my broadleafs faintly shine in the perfect calm,
smoke from the fireplace now a seamless line,
and I the dull bourgeois I would have despised:

I putter, I prune the trees, I weed the flowers.
Here of an evening in fall I'm satisfied,
sad and dumb. Everything is so ordered!
The day birds warbling goodbye, the evening ones
as yet unheard. I hear alone the implosions
and curious coos, inside, of our nursing infant.
A log shifts, fumes, brings tears, through which the
     children's
swing set, yesterday's project, glints. Time.

Time will set the concrete. The seats will be hung.
At last my daughter will climb and sway upon them,
and the baby at length. How various is pain,
how randomly shaded with joy. The single salute
of the thrush; the dove at dusk like a breathy flute;
an owl's interrogations. The dooryard darkens
and covers my trees. The ash, the hornbeam, pine.
Such mystery here, that smoke should be the constant.

Midway

. . . He asked him, "Do you see anything?" And he looked up and said, "I see men; but they look like trees, walking." Then again he laid hands upon his eyes; and he looked intently, and was restored, and saw everything clearly.

MARK 8:23–25

January.
The hours after midday are coming
back, there is time
to climb from home
to height of land for the broader vision:
north and east,
Mount Moosilauke,
its four rivers of snow conjoining;
directly west,
the little town
on the highway, all its citizens
without a doubt
preoccupied
with matters they find as grave as any;
and all around,

the traffic of beasts,
invisible now, great and tiny.
A pregnant jumble,
near and far,
then and now, in a time of year
stormy and frigid,
but I have sweated,
stripped to the waist, it has been so clear.
The dead have been dead
it seems so long,

73

and yet their ghosts are perched on every
branch above me,
cloaking themselves
in the rising vapors from my body,
the day's sole clouds.

Deep in the Sunday
village, forlorn, the sound of swings
in the empty schoolyard
clinking against
their cold steel standards, like diminished
steeple bells:
ten o'clock's
sparse service was over hours
ago. My father
lays hands on my sight
up here, and friends, and my furious brother,
who at last seems calm.
The night is losing
its sovereignty, it will not be
overlong

before it loses
its winter boast, "Come out with me,
come out and stay,
and you'll be a corpse."
The crickets, partridge, frogs will all
come back to drum
their victory;
the whippoorwills will make their hum
and click as they mate,
the freshets will loosen;
the children, done for the year with lessons,
will elect to throng
the grassy playground. . . .

The past will turn itself over, shaking
out my brother,

friends, and father,
and they will be as before, but better,
as I will be,
unless—as so often—
I'm dreaming here; unless what I sense
is just another
misty version
of lifelong longing. It's hard to say. . . .
A moment ago,
I flushed a crowd
of flying squirrels, who in their soaring
out of their holes
looked so like angels
I rubbed my eyes. And what do I see?
On the far horizon

appears to be
a line of men, there in procession . . .
as darkness deepens, they look like trees.

No Sign

What can we learn from Calvin,
a godfearing man
by his own description, but also a little insane,
as he liked to say?

You'd call him simple.
But aren't we all inclined
to believe that life revolves on radical signs?

He bought a turquoise camper,
for instance, because she was growing away—his daughter
Debbie, sixteen;
and Jimmie, eleven, was showing
hints of the adolescent estrangement coming:
the feint of a sneer,
the brows that ground together,
feet that shuffled. Now, thought Calvin, or never.

Something to hold us
at least for a while together.
The longer Calvin looked, the brighter it seemed,
the rig with its chromium trim,
its velveteen carpet,
its logo (a leaping fish)—
until at last it became incarnate Wish,
a lust at once betokened and satisfied
without a trace of guilt,
like the craving for grace
that might yet in his life be realized. . . .
Ninety a month,
after two hundred down.

His wife pretended to fume
when he drove it home,
pointing wordless to the chipped weather side
of their bungalow,
to the dent in the gravel drive
that swelled with mud. But she was the same old Lizzy
at last, and giggled.
"I know," said Cal. "I'm crazy."

The Bingo had started again at the church in May,
when they didn't need oil or wood
to heat the vestry.
The men slapped Cal on the back and shook their heads.
The women applauded
the camper's color; one said,
"like Mary's robe." Everyone laughed. One night,
Calvin and Red
and Woody took a ride
with their beers along the country roads. They all
got sentimental,
imagined a lake in fall
way up north at sunset on Calvin's behalf:
trout on the surface;
through an oxbow, the last
pillars of sun on the water; the wild loons' cackle.
"I can smell the fried fish as they sizzle,"
said Red, and friendly Woody—crude as ever—
imagined the family
"happy as hogs in manure."

Cal dropped them off and drove himself home on air.

You can't help wishing
the whole thing ended there.
It seems almost unnecessary to say

that things did not shape up exactly that way:
Debbie's a logger's mistress;
Jimmie, the boy,
is a dynamite cap of trouble.

Perhaps we should skip the intrigue,
and should keep from saying that Calvin was nuts to believe
that he could ever carry out his purpose
—bringing the family together—
with something so rootless.
For the Lord knows Calvin was rough enough on himself.
He took the camper's corrosions
as moral rebuff.
Heaven was now and forever hopeless, beyond him.
You wouldn't think
he could be so damned despondent.
Everything signalled shame: that dirty gaping
ravine in the mud,
the scars on his house's clapboard.
Calvin resorted to weeping
when he looked at Lizzy,
her hair and features fading,
the stay-at-home appearance of her clothing.

Until at last
one morning the parson selected
these words from the Gospel of Mark for his sermon's text:
"Why does this generation seek a sign?"
Whether or not
the preacher had Calvin in mind,
Calvin heard it that way.
He thought of Debbie:
what bonded him
together with her? with Jimmie?

"Truly I say to you no sign will be given"
—the Gospel quoted Jesus—"to this generation."

If there's a lesson here,
perhaps it's one
that occurred to Calvin then. It came to him
not like Revelation,
a flash of force,
but plain and simple: things will take their course.

IV

Reckoning

Reckoning

Minus twenty-five outside. Second
month, third day. Inside my child it's one
hundred and three. For five straight nights this
nameless thing (or things) has wandered in
my girl at will, and I therefore will
magic on the hand that wanders on
her forehead, my own. Perspiration
in its coursing seems so odd in this
unmoving weather. I remember
hearing of a child who crashed through ice
while skating our Unami River,
the father or mother only one
field away, which was one too many
to call back the body: remote, gray
newspaper story. And how it chilled.
One field too many. The body is
so full of many things, I'm frozen
here before it, praying for a lull:
crudely, like a man, so like a man
to exercise his fascination
with figures, to take measures, helpless
though he be: helpless—so myth has it—
as a woman. That old myth: *And which
of you by being anxious can add
one cubit to his span of life?* O,
it's not my life, but hers. I'd gladly
die. I start the thankless blasphemous
act of self-distraction: counting hairs
upon her head. I fail at forty.
I for whom the grayest terror is
profusion. If I still can number

it, it's not beyond me. I begin
again, despite the Christian doctor's
copious assurance, splendor of
ice crystals on her window at dawn
like so many amulets against
catastrophe, making of her room
a rainbow; or, outside, like soldiers,
jays who squabble over scattered seed
in sequenced shrieks. Morning takes over,
stars retreating, and the sky diffused
in the undifferentiated
blue-near-gray of thirty years ago.
We gathered in the parking lot ten
floors from great uncle in a tower
—head bald as a snowman's dented with
his knowledge, age, and hot with fever—
quaking in the hospital, while I
counted storeys, counted a hundred
autos bright with snowflakes, tried to count
the beds within the building: number
of rooms by number of floors. . . . The wards
confused me, prolix, gray with patients.
Everything appeared to multiply
past my computation—exotic
tears that all my elders were crying,
remarks let fly that, flown, kept falling:
"Uncle does nothing," said my mother,
"but tell his own telephone number,
over and over." Somebody said,
"Yesterday he made as if to knit,
calling out the stitches and the purls!"
O, he was sinking. . . . Heads bowed, motors
caught, the family disappearing now
into the incalculable throng
on the freeway. And my father, soon

to disappear himself, womanly
laying a hand upon my mother's
head, and mine. My sisters were rebuked
for "trooper's language," in their mouths so
bizarre. We were home. Tiny figures
in an ordinary tragedy.
"Still, count your blessings," each one of us
was told. And I counted all night long.
The rows of fissures in the plaster;
headlamps coursing in upon the walls
in squares; the radiator's protests,
regular, inside. These summoned me
back from all that terrified outside,
without degree or limit—tower-
tall, field-wide, and more, immeasurably—
but were no blessing, for I wandered
in that indecipherable maze,
the *idea* of the body, wherein
my cells were like my uncle's making
headway undetected; like the boy's
who drowned in that far childhood river.
Or was it a girl? I couldn't then
remember, much less now remember,
life at eighteen was already sunk
in myths and questions without number.
Why, I wondered, was I born? And why,
once born, did I turn out a man? I
put hands upon myself, but gently.
Every seed, so I had heard it said,
like every bird is tallied: nothing
falls but is accounted for somewhere.
I mark my daughter's fiery breathings.
What keeps me wakened here will keep me
present at the bed of my own seed. . . .
I feel my breasts like a mother's start

to fall, I reckon all the bristles
graying on my face. I count the charms
that I've invented in my vigil:
utterance unnumbered, ignorance
manifold as beatings of our hearts,
once to summon one loved soul from harm.

From Another Shore

—A TOAST IN MEMORY OF
DRAYTON VALENTINE

Cousin, I remember
the first drunk.

More than either of us
might say of many to follow.

Both of us fresh
off some new amorous

sorrow: you,
knees like river

weeds, down on the bank, chanting
"I Love You,

Peggy Sue," wretched whore
of a tune we loved,

it's true; I, past standing,
raising the stolen jug

and struggling up
words as if from under

the deep Atlantic, that one
last hit was left and did you want it.

The moon a mere scratch
on the blue-black gulf

of sky, but I could see
your eyes, and the dark skin

that would turn
still darker with booze

at the end, as you turned:
"Kill it," you said, and said, "By God

we have to find some girls!"
But only small fry

—giggling innocent town boys—came.
"God *damn*

a kid!" you cried,
giving lame chase.

Then the cosmic thick
conversation before unconsciousness

from which for years we would wake
proud and unsick, stars

cool swimmers over the pastures and lawns.

It was summer.
That dawn we felt we'd won one,

and at long last evening
come, we bubbled

with laughter at the tiny
radio beaming the Hour

of Revival from deepest
blackest downtown, the Reverend Melvin,

Pastor, shouting,
"I, too,

was a drifter, drenched in liquor,
till something grabbed me,

turned me *around!*"
Turn to me, first friend,

and I'll tell you something
grabbed me too.

(I have friends
who say it was God,

but I don't know,
it didn't grab you. . . .)

Time to go,
time to turn

the choir off, choiring triumph
that Pharaoh lay forever

still, his eyes gummed shut with salt.
Time to cruise

the asphalt, steaming,
violent-loined, with no one to love

except each other.
You pointed a steady

finger at the dial:
"Enough of these losers.

Kill it." The crackling
tapered off

like remotest storm.
One kills so much:

friendships, time,
the moist erotic hungers

of an August, wives, lives.
I seem to survive, and thought

I'd killed off you.
I have a couple of kids. One plays

"We Are The Champions,
My Friend." Loud and louder,

day after day.
I love him. Friend,

gone downriver
a decade, and I

turned back to dry land,
I don't know why. Somewhere

the woman you damn
near drowned in grief is raising

a daughter, my cousin,
once removed.

I don't know her name,
but think

it has Victoria in it,
or Victory.

Let's call it Victory here.
For you. For me.

Annual Report

—FOR MY WIFE

What reason to begin and end just here
—in May, the woods still rank with late gray snow
through which the jets of Adders'-tongue will show
before too long—this song about our year?
O plenty, there is plenty in this month
that marks the twelve gone by since our son's late birth:
encased; released; prostrate; now he uprears
himself on this rich festival of earth.
Tiny grace-note to you who freight with grace
this spot, and yet a miracle of growth.
May this report be my attempt to pray
he'll grow like you, and all will. May the throat
deliver words all virginal, like his.
May they seem apt as his by way of praise:

My love, what in this calendar is worst
is mine for every season. What is best,
claim for yourself; for when the infant burst
the raptor bubble of your lean long frame,
the worm that sprawls in me gave out a shriek,
a wail in his beloved Devil's name,
lament that he had found himself grown weak. . . .
In June, a month of blackflies, blooms, and gnats,
you and my daughter of seven broke the ground
for zinnia, marigold. Those canvas hats
you wore, their bug-veils drooping down,
were comic then, but now in mind appear
as things of beauty too, as if there were

in God's creation nothing beautiless.
Even the insects' wry persistent drone

comes back to me as something sweet and fine.
The gray along the toothless maw of Jess,
our old retriever, seems a kind of mantle.
He lay down on the kitchen floor, and gentle
—as he was always gentle—died. July.
The dust is fled that powdered on his grave,
the single apple sapling—Northern Spy—
I planted out of season there forms pips.
O keep the worm away, I pray, a trope
that loops through boughs, the grave, the house, the lips
of sleeping kids, your own, the studded cope
of summer night. Let all of this be saved,

and August's lake: the dawns, the mists like fountains
—grays the sun transfigured. Now forever
may I see you poised in mind against the mountain
that rims the western shore. And calling weather,
the widow loon will swim into such vision,
her cry the braver plainsong to the worm's
shrill descant of self-pity. O, girl bride,
I know myself gone by the middle season,
but I would die of grief not to have died
before you do. May God save all the children.
Yet may the mind recall as well the terms
by which it's meant to live in sanctity:
the world's "subjected to futility
not of its own will but by the will

of Him who subjected it in hope." Ah, still,
who can ignore the huff of tragedy
in the first fall gust? September:
the Northern Spy's gray fruit-lumps suddenly
small fires, and just as suddenly—remember?—
the child's opposing teeth, with which he bled
your tender breasts. You wept aloud, you said,
less for that pain than for the pain of knowing

perfection in those tiny rows of bone,
from which perfection now he'd be ungrowing.
As purest joy may flash in the mundane,
just so with woe. We thought of dentists' bills,
of wires perhaps, like those that his half-brother
must wear against a skewed and painful bite,

grid of metal-gray across such white!
We are subjected not of our own wills.
Just now at last I've mentioned the half-brother.
Is this a telling figure? Am I half-father?
My firstborn, he, who set the worm at bay
which then returned, returns. And then the daughter
sent him off. He came again. The baby
banished him once more. Can this mean I
must save myself by constant siring? Maybe,
although the beard goes gray, and slack the body.
But I was speaking of the boy, October.
Two months shy then of his thirteenth birthday,
his face and mood would suddenly turn somber
as earth when leaden autumn clouds heave over:

How I recall myself in such a season!
My father's shoulders dropping slack and round,
my mother turning mannish. The dreadful wound
and thrill of sex and self-preoccupation.
The world, just now all springtime, in a blink
a seamless, dreary, flat and chill November.
The boy's eyes flooding gray. . . . I know I think
I know his thoughts, though "thought" is not the word;
who would impute it to the self-willed member,
evil's root as much as filthy lucre,
shape- and soul-mate of the filthy worm?
And yet an organ of sincerest pleasure. . . .

It seems that I, in wandering mazes lost,
proceed by warring halves. Is that the cost

to one who seeks to front "futility"
as Paul construed it for the Roman churchmen?
Is "hope" its mocking earthly avatar?
Are all the impassioned songs and poems to women
made by lonely men a litany
whose hidden theme is gloomier by far
than they may think? the intercourse they beg
by way of overcoming cheerless halfness
—figured in decembral chill and fog,
not clarity nor yet true thrilling storm—
no intercourse at all? If so, we're hapless.
(I hear the faint sick murmur of the worm.)
Oh, put it off! The children all were born,

and if the sudden plunge of January,
freezing bone, suggested vanity,
didn't the sun come on to melt the gray
of rime from windows, and indeed the hills
show clearer then than ever? One could see
the valiant buds begin their yearly pull
against what seemed damnation. And can't I
—good coffee perking, infant sprawled in bed—
pull equally? Your laughter fills each room.
How do you do it? Life-love, teach me how.
"Is that," you whisper, pointing to the stairs
down which my sleepyheaded daughter treads,
"an emblem of futility and doom?"
I'll make of this whatever I allow. . . .

In mind, the school bus was a mobile jonquil,
giant bud in February's gray.
Because of you, these bursts into the tranquil.

Because of you, not least of all your ear
(I have already credited your eye)
for valiant things: our neighbor said last year,
so you remind me, of his rabbit hound,
"He's got so old he has to lean against
a bank to howl." The hound is in the ground,
the neighbor too, so soon our time is spent.
And yet the two survive by dint of will,
theirs then, yours now. I give our pup a pill
to quell his worm. (If only a pill quelled mine!)
As the children's school bus ambles off, it shines.

March, as fits the proverb, came like lions
and out it went, all lambs, at least in color:
a late snow powdered every inch of lawn,
but when we looked around was gone. A flower
—lily—poked its tongue beneath a gray,
steaming hulk of stump, around which played
springtails, or snowfleas as we call them here.
Imagine them, such tiny signs of life
against all odds, about to end their year,
as we shall too, my very perfect wife.
Vermicular, they seem, but innocent
as those great moths that bear a question mark
upon each wing, come softly in the dark,
their question, maybe, Why not be content,

why not affirm by will what is? In April,
they clustered thick as fleece upon the screens,
the evening dark itself grown soft. My dreams
of piercing through the gray of mystery
on earth seem idle. Now, the year's full circle:
cased blossoms bursting from the apple tree,
the prostrate dog now grass, one son a man,
a daughter who like you grows beautiful,

an infant who has found a way to stand,
the worm entombed as if beneath a mountain,
this spot of ground a fête of resurrection,
since what is hope if not futility
for moments stood on end? My love, it's May,
first month of our obscure divinity,

creator, creature, riddle, lover, maid.

The Contemporary Poetry Series

EDITED BY PAUL ZIMMER

The Contemporary Poetry Series

EDITED BY BIN RAMKE

J. T. Barbarese, *Under the Blue Moon*
Richard Cole, *The Glass Children*
Wayne Dodd, *Sometimes Music Rises*
Sydney Lea, *No Sign*
Gary Margolis, *Falling Awake*
Aleda Shirley, *Chinese Architecture*
Susan Stewart, *The Hive*
Terese Svoboda, *All Aberration*